TWENTY-ONE

VIEWS IN BELFAST

AND ITS NEIGHBOURHOOD

ST. ANNE'S CHURCH

DUBLIN:

PHILIP DIXON HARDY, 3, CECILIA-STREET,

AND W. F. WAKEMAN, D'OLIER-STREET.

LONDON: RICHARD GROOMBRIDGE, 6, PANYER-ALLEY, PATERNOSTER-ROW.

EDINBURGH: FRASER AND CO.

1837.

Price 2s. 6d.

TWENTY-ONE VIEWS
IN BELFAST
AND ITS NEIGHBOURHOOD

TWENTY-ONE

VIEWS IN BELFAST

AND ITS NEIGHBOURHOOD

DUBLIN:

PHILIP DIXON HARDY, 3, CECILIA-STREET.

LONDON: RICHARD GROOMBRIDGE, 6, PANYER-ALLEY, PATERNOSTER-ROW.

1836.

TWENTY-ONE VIEWS IN BELFAST
AND ITS NEIGHBOURHOOD

(DUBLIN, 1837)

Edited by P D HARDY

Reprinted, with notes and an introduction by

C E B BRETT

LINEN HALL LIBRARY

jointly with the

ULSTER ARCHITECTURAL HERITAGE SOCIETY

BELFAST
2005

First published 2005
by the
Linen Hall Library
17 Donegall Square North, Belfast BT1 5GB
jointly with the
Ulster Architectural Heritage Society
66 Donegall Pass, Belfast BT7 1BU

Edited by Gordon Wheeler
Designed by Della Varilly
Printed by Nicholson & Bass

ISBN 1 900921 35 9

A catalogue record for this book is available from the British Library

Front and back endpapers: Text taken from original paper covers dated 1837
Frontispiece: Original title page dated 1836

Contents

Introduction

THIS BOOK reproduces a collection of views of Belfast commissioned for, and said by the editor, Philip Hardy, never to have been actually printed in, the *Dublin Penny Journal*, and published in book form, at the (then) astronomical price of two shillings and sixpence: compared with the penny price of the journal in its original form. The Journal had been founded in 1832 by Caesar Otway, George Petrie, and John O'Donovan. It is described by Tom Clyde as "A very attractive popular journal which is liberally illustrated with engravings of the Irish landscape, maps and diagrams, the quality of these is further improved after 1834 when a new steam printing press was ordered from Glasgow...The quantity and quality of illustrations, the use of the latest technology to keep the price down, the wide distribution...and the large circulation...all declare that we are firmly into the new age of greatly improved communications and mass readership" *(Irish literary magazines).*

It was a high-minded venture. In 1833, when the first bound volume for the previous year was issued, its Conductors – as they chose to call themselves – laid it down: "Agreeing...with its valuable predecessors only in the exclusion of politics and sectarian religion, and in the general desire to be useful and instructive, the PENNY JOURNAL started on new and exclusively national ground, and with national as well as useful objects in view. The subjects chiefly chosen were such as were most likely to attract the attention of the Irish people, next to those of politics and polemics... namely, the history, biography, poetry, antiquities, natural history, legends and traditions of the country".

Of the original Conductors, the Rev. Caesar Otway (1780–1842) was a popular preacher but never attained advancement in the Church of Ireland; of him it was written, somewhat elliptically, that "he was the centre of the young literature of the Irish capital, and he laboured to prevent its assuming that sectarian character in the hands of others which unfortunately was too manifest in his own" (Webb, quoting *The Athenaeum*). George Petrie (1790–1866) and John O'Donovan (1809–1861) were the acknowledged intellectual giants of Irish scholarship in the first half of the nineteenth century.

But, their successor, Philip Dixon Hardy, was by no means of the same intellectual calibre. Hayley regards him as publishing "a cheap and snippety ragbag of extracts". However, on the credit side, the Journal reached a circulation of 40,000 in a population of eight million: and in its best weeks, even 50,000 copies. It seems that Hardy was indeed a most unreliable editor. In the first place, the number of views included in this little book was actually twenty-three, not twenty-one; the two extras appear to be the general views of Belfast after Andrew Nicholl, who executed a large number of water-colour views of Belfast and its Long Bridge from slightly differing angles. Then, Hardy's statement that the views had not previously been printed was highly misleading: for seven of them had appeared in a seven-page supplement to the first, 1833, volume, costing two pence; another seven had appeared in a nine-page supplement to the fourth, 1836, volume, apparently again for two pence; and seven of the prints reproduced in this book had been used in volumes 1 and 2 of the Journal itself.

Nevertheless, perhaps because of the vast disparity in pricing, the book here reprinted seems to be of the utmost rarity: how many copies were originally printed is not known; but only three, one of them incomplete, appear to survive in public collections: there is, of course, no means of knowing what other copies may survive in private hands. There is one copy, but lacking its title-page, in the National Library of Ireland, Dublin; one complete copy in the Bodleian Library, Oxford; and the copy from which this edition is reproduced in the Linen Hall Library, Belfast, bearing the signature of Lavens M. Ewart, a scion of of the well-known Belfast linen family, and local historian. Why so few copies have survived is not clear. They were extremely expensive. There are other curious discrepancies concerning this little publication: the date on the title-page is 1836; whilst the editor's prefatory note is dated from Dublin, 1837, and the front cover also bears the date 1837, which was certainly the real date of its publication.

Of the artists employed for these twenty-three views, Andrew Nicholl (1804–1886) was one of the leading painters of his day, son of a bootmaker of Church Lane, Belfast; he was one of the earliest contributors to the *Dublin Penny Journal*; two of his contributions here are known to have been engraved by Brandon and Wright. Of the other engravers, Robert and Samuel Clayton were both brought up by their father Benjamin as wood-engravers; both worked for the Journal; both ended up by emigrating to New South Wales, where Samuel prospered, but Robert proved "idle and a ne'er-do-well" (Strickland). Horatio Nelson was a Dublin miniature-painter who did jobbing engraving of woodcuts to help eke out a living.

In 1834, the Journal had changed ownership, passing from the learned Petrie and O'Donovan into the hands of Philip Dixon Hardy (1793–1875), "the printer, publisher, proprietor and editor of so many Irish magazines", but a considerably less scholarly and high-minded proprietor than his predecessors. In 1836, he decided to close it down, pleading ill-health as his reason. But this may not have been the principal, certainly not the only, reason; for, according to Barbara Hayley, "the paper was doomed by a reference to 'the bloody reign of Mary' which infuriated the Catholic hierarchy, who founded the *Catholic Penny Magazine*, taking away a readership of 6,000 straight away". (A notable example, surely, of the proverbial Irish 'belt with a crozier'.)

I am indebted to Gordon Wheeler for the following extracts from an article, 'Old popular pennyworths', by one James Hayes, which appeared in the *Irish Book Lover* of May 1911. "The great success of the "Penny Magazine", founded by Lord Brougham and Charles Knight, inspired Caesar Otway and George Petrie – the one a writer of acknowledged ability, the other a first rate artist and antiquary – to produce a similar work in Ireland, "with national as well as useful objects in view." They had many initial difficulties to contend with, but, these surmounted, the first number of the DUBLIN PENNY JOURNAL appeared on Saturday, 30th June, 1832. It was an eight page quarto printed by J. S. Folds, illustrated with wood engravings by Clayton from sketches by Petrie, and issued in weekly numbers, monthly parts at fivepence, and annual volumes at five shillings. It contained biographies and portraits of distinguished natives, legends and folk-lore committed to print for the first time, interesting topographical views, and in the words of Mr. D. J. O'Donoghue, "made known to the world the priceless value and extent of the material records in stone and metals, no less than in manuscript" existing in our land. Its verse was above the average, for in it, Mangan, posing as an Italian, commenced his mystifications with so-called translations from foreign tongues.... The twentieth number boasted of a circulation of forty thousand; the critical journals were loud in their praise; and Southey, the poet laureate said, he "prized it as the most valuable in his library." Yet somehow it was not a financial success, for at the end of the first year, the projectors found themselves in debt to the printer, to the extent of £1,700 ! They therefore transferred it to Philip Dixon Hardy, who being printer, publisher and editor, was able to continue it at less expense. So from No. 57 until the end, three years later, it bears his imprint. But its glory had departed, for, to quote Mr. O'Donoghue again, "everyone in Dublin knew that the journal was doomed to extinction as soon as this fanatical swaddler assumed control. He had already compassed the death of one or two other journals, and nearly all its distinguished writers ceased to take any further interest." Its latest numbers ceased to be either national or useful and it died ingloriously in June, 1836". A swaddler, it seems, was a derogatory Anglo-Irish slang term for any Protestant.

The original slight booklet, now (as remarked above) exceptionally rare, is reproduced, with Hardy's historical essay, and his notes on the illustrations; but the illustrations themselves – wood engravings for the most part – have been somewhat enlarged from an average block size of about 145 x 110 mm, and allowed a full page each, with first, Hardy's notes, then some additional notes by the present editor, on the facing page. Also, their order has been slightly changed, so that all the illustrations of the town of Belfast appear first, then those of scenes in County Down, then those of scenes in County Antrim.

From an architectural-historical point of view, it may be remarked that this booklet very clearly marks the final dominance of the classical style, especially amongst the Presbyterian churches, in the years just before the emergence, under the influence of Pugin and others, of the Victorian Gothic Revival. But that is only right and proper; for its publication only antedates the accession of the youthful Queen Victoria by a couple of years, if that. It is perhaps best regarded as a survey of the 'Modern' architecture of Belfast and district in 1835: taking 'Modern' to mean, 'of the past fifty years'.

But, the times were beginning to change; note the observations of Colonel de Montmorency on the Gothic style at Shane's Castle, on page 54. The changeover from classical to gothical was to take a few more years. In 1842, Lawson could still write "the Belfastians appear to have a mortal antipathy to steeples or spires of any description. Several of the Presbyterian places of worship are elegant edifices, and have very considerable architectural pretensions, but they want spires, which would have been a great *set-off* to the town, and are rather heavily furnished with porticoes, which diminish their effect as buildings". And in the following year, Thackeray wrote "The stranger cannot fail to be struck (and haply a little frightened) by the great number of meeting-houses that decorate the town, and give evidence of great sermonizing on Sundays. These buildings do not affect the Gothic, like many of the meagre edifices of the Established and the Roman Catholic churches, but have a physiognomy of their own – a thick-set citizen look. Porticoes have they, to be sure, and ornaments Doric, Ionic, and what-not: but the meeting-house peeps through all these classical friezes and entablatures." That was soon to change: between the 1850s and the 1950s, the skyline was dominated by a profusion of Gothic spires and steeples, competing for notice with factory chimneys. Today, alas, both are completely overshadowed by characterless high-rise blocks of offices or flats: and it seems that, as one falls, another springs up to take its place.

C E B Brett
March 2005

BRIEF HISTORICAL RECORD OF THE TOWN OF BELFAST [1837]

The town of Belfast confessedly ranks the third in Ireland, yielding in importance but to Dublin and Cork; and from the rapid increase in the number of inhabitants, and the extensive additions which are daily making both of private and public buildings, as well as from that spirit of improvement and enterprize which charcacterizes its inhabitants generally, there is every prospect that it will, in a very few years, become the second town in the kingdom, as to extent, commerce, manufactures, and wealth–to which we may also add literature. This prosperous and wealthy town, distinguished no less for its commerce and manufacture, than for its cultivation of literature and science, is situated at the mouth of the river Lagan, which falls into the sea at the extremity of the bay, anciently called Carrickfergus Lough, but which is now often designated as the Lough of Belfast. Though the period of this town's first attaining any degree of commercial consequence is well known, its origin is now lost in impenetrable obscurity. Conjecture, indeed, founded upon its locality, would lead us to suppose that it took its rise from an obscure and mean village placed at a ford which formed the principal point of communication between the northern parts of the counties of Down and Antrim. Although in its vicinity there are some lofty hills, and especially a very considerable range to the northwest, yet from the low situation in which the town itself is built, its appearance, from a distance, is not only unimpressive, but mean, and it is not til the stranger almost enters it that he is convinced of its extent, commercial importance and wealth. The prospect which presents itself from the town, in the direction of the shore and the long range of mountains, is peculiarly fine, uniting much natural sublimity with numerous artificial beauties–the Lough, which divides the counties of Down and Antrim, and which at its entrance is about five miles broad, narrowing gradually towards Belfast, is bounded on the left by the lofty coast of Antrim, and on the right by the shore of the county of Down, and is on either side decorated with handsome villas and whitened cottages–the sloping hills finely cultivated, and the more lofty eminences presenting a pleasing variety of surface; the shipping in the bay and along the coast adding greatly to the picturesque appearance which the entire presents.

A castle appears to have been erected here at an early period of the occupation of Ulster by the English, supposed to have been founded by the well known John de Courcey, to whom this part of Ireland was allotted, or by some of his followers. No historical record of its foundation, however, is to be found. It seems to have been held by the English in connexion with the castle of Carrickfergus, a strong hold of vastly greater grandeur and importance, and their extensive possessions in the part of the county of Down called the Ards. The first mention in history of Belfast relates to its destruction by Edward le Bruce, who, invited by O'Neil and other Irish chieftains, came over to Ireland in 1315, with 6000 men, and devastated the northern parts of the English pale, which, according to Spencer, then extended to Dunluce. Among the good towns and strong holds belonging to the English which he wasted and sacked, was Belfast, which thus fell into the hands of the Irish, who long after continued to hold undisturbed possession of almost the entire of Ulster, the attention of the English nation being diverted by the civil wars of the Roses, as well as by their French expeditions, from attempting to regain their lost possessions in the North of Ireland.

In the reign of Henry VIII. Gerald, Earl of Kildare, then Lord Deputy, finding it necessary to check the growing power of the O'Neils, made several expeditions into Ulster; in one of which, in 1503, he took the castle of Belfast, but unable to hold his ground there, he dismantled it before his return to Dublin. This is the first distinct historical mention of the castle. Upon his retreat it was again repaired and occupied by the Irish, till in 1512, it was once more taken and destroyed by the same Earl of Kildare. In 1552, the Lord Deputy, Sir James Crofts, fortified the castle and garrisoned it. At this time its seems probable that the outworks were erected, considerable traces of which remained until a few years ago. They do not appear, however, to have consisted of any regular fortifications, but merely strong earthen ramparts and a deep fosse. To the custody of Hugh Mac Neil Oge, of Clan-hugh-boy, the castle was soon after confided, upon his swearing allegiance to the Crown of England; but he having soon after lost his life in a conflict which took place with a body of Scots, who made a predatory descent on the neighbouring coast, Randolphus Lane, an Englishman was next appointed to the command of the castle; but the possession of the surrounding territory by the descendants of O'Neil, continued until, in 1571, Elizabeth made a grant to Sir Thomas Smith and Thomas Smith his son, of a considerable tract of country, within the territories of Claneboy and the Great Ards, which had been vested in the Crown by act of Parliament for the attainder of Shane O'Neil. Of this grant the particulars are fully given in a valuable manuscript called–"The Grand Inquisition of the County of Down," taken in 1621. In it the castle of Belfast is included with several others. The inquisition recites that "in the Queen's earldom of Ulster, there be divers parcels of land that be waste, or inhabited with a wicked, barbarous and uncivil people, some Scottish, and some wild Irish;" and that "the Smiths, with a power of Englishmen, agree to subdue all, and them plant with faithful subjects." It then recites various covenants on the part of the Smiths, to the effect that all the adventurers who accompanied them should have certain portions of land, on certain tenures; that they (the Smiths) should have for every plow-land, one able English foot-soldier, well armed and furnished like the men of England; or for every two townlands, a light English horseman, accoutred in the same manner; and that on fifteen days' notice they should appear before the Deputy at every general hostings, with a third part of all the horsemen and footmen they were bound to provide; that they should grant no estate to any of the mere Irish or Scottish Irish, nor intermarry with them without permission. The Inquisition then states that Thomas Smith, the son, did, in 1572, enter the earldom of Ulster, but did not subdue it. It then proceeds to allege the violation of the various covenants in the grant, and the non-payment of the Crown rent; and that, therefore, the whole grant reverted to the king (James I.)

It is a remarkable proof of the slight importance that Belfast had attained previous to 1586, that in Hollinshed's Chronicle, printed in London in that year, there is no mention whatever made of it in the enumeration of the chief towns and havens of the counties of Down and Antrim, among which are mentioned more than one which at this day are mere fishing villages.

Many forfeitures having taken place about the close of the 16th century, in the northern counties of Ireland, extensive plans were brought into operation by James I. and his ministers, for the settlement and plantation of them. The Lord Deputy, Sir Arthur Chichester, having been most active in forwarding the King's views, was rewarded by considerable grants of land, and "as a further mark of his Majesty's lasting favour, he did, by letters patent, bearing date at Westminster, 23rd February, 1612, create him Baron of Belfast." In the year following a charter was granted to Belfast, constituting it a corporation, consisting of a sovereign, twelve burgesses, and commonalty, with the privilege of sending two members to Parliament. From this period may Belfast date its rise, not only in political but also in commercial importance: the latter, however, received decisive assistance from the purchase by Lord Strafford, on the part of the Crown, from the Corporation of Carrickfergus, in

1637, of their privilege of receiving one-third of the duties payable on goods imported into that town, and other extensive monopolies which it enjoyed; in consequence of which the trade of Carrickfergus rapidly transferred itself from thence to Belfast. The unsettled state of the country during the succeeding years, and the well known rebellion of 1641, greatly retarded the advancing improvement of the town; which was successively occupied, during the contest of Charles I. and his Parliament, by the Scottish troops under General Monroe, and the Parliament forces under the celebrated General Monk. From them it was re-taken by the Royalists by stratagem; and shortly after the arrival of Cromwell in Ireland in 1649, and the subsequent reduction of Drogheda, he sent Colonel Venables to reduce Belfast, which, after a resistance of four days, surrendered to him, having thus sustained four sieges, and as many times changed masters, in the lapse of not more than six years.

In 1688, a new charter was issued by James II. in which the number of burgesses was increased to thirty-five, and the privileges of the Corporation were much abridged; a power being vested in the chief governor and the privy council of removing a sovereign, burgess, or other officer at pleasure. In reference to the political part which Belfast took in the great struggle which terminated in the establishment of William the III. upon the throne of these kingdoms, it is enough to say, that in this town the cause of James was by no means popular, and the arrival of Duke Schomberg, in 1690, was hailed with joy. On the 9th of June following, William himself landed at Carrickfergus, from whence he proceeded immediately to Belfast, where he was received with enthusiasm, and remained there nearly a week, being lodged in the house of Sir William Franklin; the site of which is now occupied by an old established hotel, the Donegal Arms.

The advantages derived from tranquillity soon began to manifest themselves in the increased prosperity of Belfast, which from this period advanced with rapid strides to the place it now holds among the commercial towns of Ireland. Its history, for many succeeding years, presents few striking incidents; but it is quite obvious that this is by no means inconsistent with advancement in population, in trade, and in wealth. In the spring of 1692, seven arches of the Long Bridge fell in, it having been much shaken by the drawing of the heavy cannon of the Duke of Schomberg over it. This bridge, the foundation of which had been laid in 1682, but the completion of which was delayed for several years after by the unsettled state of the country, is generally supposed to occupy the site of the ancient ford across the Lagan, from which, as we have before mentioned, Belfast is said to have had its origin. The bridge consists of twenty-one arches, and is 2562 feet in length. It has long been in a tottering condition, and its final removal, and the substitution of a modern one in its place, has long been contemplated. In 1706, the castle of Belfast was destroyed by fire, by the carelessness of a servant, and three daughters of Arthur, third earl of Donegal, unfortunately perished in the flames. Till lately some vestiges of the castle were to be seen, but now all trace of it has vanished, and its site is chiefly occupied by a fish and vegetable market. It is thus described by an English gentleman, who visited Ireland in 1635:–"At Belfast, my Lord Chichester hath a dainty stately palace, which is indeed the glory and beauty of that town, where he is mostly resident."

The descent of the French squadron under Thurot, in 1760, and his occupation of Carrickfergus, naturally excited great alarm in Belfast, which it was his intention to have entered and plundered; but some delay having been fortunately occasioned by a difference of opinion with his colleague, M. Flobert, the inhabitants of the town and the neighbouring district rapidly got under arms, a body of troops were quickly despatched to their aid, and the excellent Lord Charlemont, as Governor of the County of Armagh, proceeded to take the command of the militia of that county. The result was, that Thurot was obliged to abandon the enterprise, and re-embark; the three frigates composing his little squadron were afterwards captured or dispersed before they could get out of the Irish channel. From the apprehension of a repetition of such attempts upon the part of the French nation to make descents upon the coast, arose the celebrated military associations known as the Volunteers; but it was not, however, till the year 1778, that these associations assumed a definite shape and name. In their formation Belfast took a leading and distinguished part; and here were held some reviews of the entire Volunteer force of the North of Ireland, upon a scale of great magnitude and splendour.

At the earlier period of the memorable French Revolution, a powerful sensation was produced in Belfast, where it was hailed by many as the dawn of a new era in the history of the civil and religious interests of mankind. Imbued with an ardent love of liberty, they were caught by the enthusiasm of the day, and until undeceived by the frightful scenes of bloodshed which rapidly followed, they hailed the progress of the revolutionists with unrestrained demonstration of the liveliest sympathy and joy. Addresses to the French nation, expressive of these feelings, were rapidly prepared, and numerously and respectably signed. The fermented state of the public mind consequent upon these proceedings, affords, we think, the clue to the formation in Belfast of the secret societies, so well known afterwards by the designation of the United Irishmen. The government, whose subversion they sought to effect, took active measures in self-defence, for their suppression, and, in consequence, Belfast was visited by many of the calamities necessarily resulting from the steps taken to provide against the anticipated conspiracy. Many arrests took place, and martial law was proclaimed. At length the rebellion of 1798 broke out; but we learn that to such a state of subjection were the conspirators here reduced by the unremitting vigilance and exertion of the civil and military powers, that, while insurrection was blazing forth in various parts of Ireland, not the slightest commotion betrayed itself here. The lapse of a few years restored peace to this distracted country; and Belfast once more resumed her rapid progress to her present state of commercial prosperity, which no untoward events have since occurred to interrupt.

Of the amazing rapidity with which Belfast has of late years been advancing to its present degree of importance, a tolerably fair estimate may be formed from the following statement:–From a plan of the town, which is supposed to have been taken about twenty years after the rebellion of 1641, it appears that it consisted at that time of five small streets, the houses in which are imagined to have been principally built of wood, surrounded by an earthen rampart of great solidity, and by a deep fosse or ditch, having outworks and bastions of very considerable strength. There were two gates or entrances, the west gate and the north gate–the former standing where Chapel Lane is now situated, the latter at the junction of North-street and Hercules-street. To these were affixed drawbridges and out-works. This fortification or rampart was nearly a mile in circuit, and enclosed that space of ground on which North-street, Hercules-street, High-street, Bridge-street, Waring-street, Skipper-street, Church-lane, Anne-street, and Corn-market, still stand. In 1760 the town did not contain more than about 1800 houses, and between 8000 and 9000 inhabitants; and, until within the period we have mentioned, the houses in all parts of the town were of rather a poor description, many of those in Bridge-street having roofs thatched with straw. The river, which runs through High-street, was uncovered in its entire length and, although walled in on either side, and having five bridges across it, was, nevertheless, a great inconvenience to the inhabitants; and, notwithstanding it was at different times, in different lengths, covered over, the street has, comparatively speaking, only recently assumed the appearance which it now presents. Not very many years since, it was the favourite resort of a number of pedlars, who had their various commodities ranged along it, in the same manner as they continue still to expose their wares for sale on market and fair days in the surrounding towns.

Sixty or seventy years ago there were few public buildings of any account; but several elegant edifices, recently erected, give a pleasing aspect to the place, by taking away much of that uniform stiffness which for a length of time characterised its appearance, in consequence of there being so many brick buildings without any intervention of stone-work. It has much the appearance of an English town, in the number and variety of its houses of divine worship, in its many handsome and well-assorted shops, and the indications of business evinced in the bustle and activity of the inhabitants, passing and repassing the streets, which are marked by great regularity, having very good foot-ways, and being, in general, well cleansed and lighted. The quays and docks are extensive and convenient–one graving dock being capable of containing three vessels of two hundred tons each, and the other a much larger number of vessels of a superior class. The merchants' stores erected along the quays are also extensive.

By the last census, viz. that of 1831, the number of dwelling houses is stated to be 8,710; and the population, males 25,450, females 28,287; total 53,737. It is to be observed, that this is exclusive of the populous suburb of Ballymacarrett, which (though in the county of Down, and separated from Belfast Proper by the river Lagan, across which the communication is at present carried on by means of the Long Bridge of which we have already spoken) may, we think, be fairly considered as part of the town of Belfast. The census of 1831 states that the population of Ballymacarrett to be, males 2,490, females 2,678; total 5,168. The relative proportion of Protestants to Roman Catholics in Belfast cannot be stated with precision; but we are informed that the present Roman Catholic population is estimated at 20,000.

The places of public worship are in number twenty-one, of which three are of the Established Church, namely, the church of St. Anne's, a Chapel-of-ease, and a Free Church, lately built; six belong to the Presbyterian body–two of these are of what is termed the New-light; there are four meeting-houses of Methodist congregations; three of the Seceders; one of the Independents; one of the Covenanters; one of the Society of Friends; and two Roman Catholic chapels. In Ballymacarrett there is a parish church, a Roman Catholic chapel, and a Methodist meeting-house.

The customs in 1688, were estimated at £20,000; in 1832, they amounted to £210,177.16s.6d.

The founderies for the casting of iron and metal are on an extensive scale; and the manufacture of glass, salt, vitriol, and other less important matters, is by no means inconsiderable. But the chief manufacture is that of cotton, which is comparatively of recent introduction into this country, having been first brought to Belfast about the end of the last century. It now gives employment to a great mass of the population in this town, and the surrounding district; and has in great measure superseded the weaving of linen, at least in the houses of the peasantry. There can be no doubt but that the domestic manufacture of linen has greatly retrograded of late years; but notwithstanding, we have learned from a source of unquestionable authority, that by the recent erection of flax-mills, and public establishments for the manufacture of linens, the export trade has now regained its former extent, and, in fact, was never greater than at the present day.

It is worthy of observation, that as far as machinery is concerned, a poor-house was the cradle of the present cotton trade of Ireland. The early introduction of a manufacture, already of immense and increasing importance, has been traced to the perseverance of private individuals, actuated by a wish to create useful employment for destitute children–to assist the working classes at a time when the linen manufacture was in a most depressed state–and to render a permanent benefit to the community at large. A circumstance which should be a stimulus to the exertions of every individual, as it demonstrates how much may be effected by a limited capital and ardent zeal. There are now eight large cotton mills in full work in Belfast and its neighbourhood.

There are several Banks, namely, the Belfast Banking Company, and the Northern Banking Company, the capital of each of which is £500,000; the Ulster Bank, and the Agricultural and Commercial Bank; a branch of the Bank of Ireland, and one of the Provincial Bank of Ireland.

Of the literary establishments, the first in rank is the Belfast Academical Institution, in which a comprehensive system of education of youth is carried on under a body incorporated by Act of Parliament in 1810. Another of high character is the Belfast Academy, instituted 25th January, 1786. There are besides various literary societies which meet periodically, the Belfast Natural History Society, and a Mechanic's Institute; also a Society for the protection of the Fine Arts, called "The Belfast Association of Irish Artists."

The first edition of the Bible ever printed in Ireland, appeared from the press of James Blow, in Belfast, in the year 1704; and the Belfast Newsletter is (with the single exception of, we believe, a Limerick paper) the oldest newspaper in Ireland, having been established in 1737. The other newspapers published here, are, the Commercial Chronicle, the Mercantile Register, the Northern Whig, and the Ulster Times.

St Anne's Church

Which we have given as a vignette in the title page, is situated in Donegal-street. It is the parish church, and was erected in the year 1778. It has a handsome Doric portico, and an Ionic tower, of considerable height, with a Corinthian cupola, which is of copper, the tower being formed of wood.

THE old Corporation Church in High Street was demolished as structurally dangerous in 1774. Work on the new parish church was actually completed at a cost of £10,000 in 1776, and (for once) was paid for at the sole expense of the fifth Earl of Donegall. When he was aged only 21, in February 1761, he bought the Elizabethan manor-house of Fisherwick, in Staffordshire (now demolished), and in 1766 employed Capability Brown to build him a vast Palladian mansion, with a great Corinthian portico, and to lay out an extensive park. It was no doubt because of his Staffordshire connections that, a few years after the completion of Fisherwick in 1774, he brought in Francis Hiorne of Warwick to design St Anne's: though whether Hiorne ever actually came over to Belfast is an open question. He was apparently a specialist in gingerbread-Gothick, of which Tetbury parish church, in Gloucestershire, remains a good example. It had originally been intended that the church should be dedicated to St Patrick: but it was eventually named for St Anne in honour of Lord Donegall's first wife, Lady Anne Hamilton, daughter of the Duke of Hamilton.

Despite Hiorne's predilection for the Gothick, the church, as is evident from the wood engraving, by Nelson and Bruce, was in a classical style, described by Samuel Lewis in 1837 as "consisting of a nave and chancel, with a lofty Ionic tower surmounted by a Corinthian cupola covered with copper, forming an interesting and conspicuous object for many miles around". The upper part of the tower was made of painted wood; unfortunately, it proved too unsafe to hang a bell; and the original porch-like low portico was taken down and rebuilt in its taller Corinthian form in 1832, subsequently modified by the addition of a pediment in place of the central balustrade. This perhaps explains, at least in part, the discrepancy between Hardy's description of the building, the orders indicated in the somewhat crude engraving, Samuel Lewis's description, and John Thomson's steel engraving of 1823 used by Benn in his History of Belfast. It seems likely that the actual building work was supervised by Roger Mulholland, carpenter turned architect, who developed the surrounding streets for Lord Donegall. The church was demolished in the early months of 1904 to make way for the new St Anne's cathedral, having remained in use standing, pathetically without its tower, until the last moment, inside the skeleton of the much larger new building.

The White Linen Hall

An extensive range of building, situated in Donegal-square, completely surrounded by a handsome railing, on a low brick wall, coped with stone. The area between the railing and the building being tastefully planted with evergreens, and flowering shrubs, affords a most agreeable promenade for the inhabitants at all seasons. The interior of the building is fitted up with different offices and rooms for the factors, and is particularly well calculated for the purposes for which it was designed.

It was the linen, not the market hall, that was white. This was a very large building, of two storeys, 382 feet long by 282 feet deep externally, the main façade being 27 bays long, for which the site was granted by Lord Donegall on 4th September 1783 to four Trustees – George Black, William Legg, John Russell, and Francis Turnley. Subscriptions raised towards the building amounted to £17,550. There was a central pedimented block with a tall quoined entrance archway and a subsidiary block with three-light Venetian windows at either side of it. The windows on the inside of the entrance block had Gibbsian surrounds. A grant of additional ground was made in 1803. It is very likely, although no conclusive proof has so far turned up, that Roger Mulholland was both architect and builder of the Linen Hall. It was unusual in eighteenth-century Irish linen markets in not having open arcades where purchasers could inspect the bolts of linen in full daylight; considered unduly plain for such a central and important building, a cupola, possibly of wood, with clock and weathervane, was added in 1815.

The internal arrangements of the building are unclear, apart from the fact that the library of the Belfast Society for Promoting Knowledge moved into the central upstairs room in 1802, free of rent. Unfortunately, in July 1885 one of the weights of the clock in the cupola, weighing five hundredweight, crashed through the ceiling of the central reading room in the middle of the night. An old photograph of the Magazine Room of the library shows a very heavily coved cornice, and a fine marble chimneypiece with Ionic columns. In 1808, 1812, 1817, 1818, 1844, 1868, and 1872 the library was accorded additional space, as the needs of the original merchants gradually decreased. But in 1888, the Countess of Shaftesbury, successor of the Donegalls, expressed her wish to reacquire the whole site, and then regrant it to the Belfast Corporation for the building of the new City Hall. In 1892, the library removed to its new premises on the north side of the Square, taking with it the now customary name of Linen Hall Library; in 1898 the old buildings were demolished; in 1906, the new and splendid building on their site was finally completed.

NELSON DEL
R. CLAYTON. SC.

Academical Institution

The edifice erected for this Institution is an extensive range of building, surrounded by a wall, with an iron railing in front, situated at the western end of the town, apparently designed to form the centre of a square, on three sides of which, houses, many of them of a very elegant description, have already been erected. The building itself, however, though presenting rather a good front, is by no means of that architectural character which such an institution would demand.

[⁂ Since the Engravings were worked off, we have been informed of the following errors in the names of the Buildings, by the Artist who sketched them: - "The Institution" should be called "The Royal College"]

'INST.', as it is universally known, is now the only surviving work in Ireland of that great architect, Sir John Soane; although it is but a very pale reflection of his original scheme. Lord Donegall agreed to provide a generous, flat, four-acre site at the head of Chichester Street. Soane was approached for plans in 1808 by Adam McClean on behalf of the newly-formed Management Committee, which projected a highly ambitious scheme combining the functions of a school and a university college. Soane responded with truly noble plans, offering his services free. His scheme, in a multi-columnar neo-classical manner, proposed three long ranges, of descending degrees of grandeur, with linking blocks, two broad internal quadrangles, open squares at either side, and a long arcaded rear wall along the western boundary of the site. This was far beyond the funds at the disposal of the Committee. Although £10,000 had been raised locally in the first fortnight, no support was forthcoming from government. In the event, though no less than forty-six of Soane's drawings survive, only a much simplified version of the most modest range at the rear was actually built. It is of brown brick, of three storeys and twenty-three bays, with a central recessed porch borne on two Doric columns, four pairs of giant stucco pilasters, recessed round-headed windows on the ground floor, and a niche over the main entrance: unhappily, this has been filled in, so depriving the façade of a much-needed plastic feature. Thomson's engraving of 1823 in Benn's *History of Belfast* shows a central bell-cote on the roof, probably never in fact built.

The foundations were laid in July, 1810; work proceeded rather slowly due to shortages caused by Napoleon's Continental Blockade; the school opened its doors to pupils on 1st February, 1814. One of their number was George Benn, later to be the historian of Belfast, who noted "The grounds, the building, and all the surroundings which the boys beheld...were dreary looking. The ground was wet and swampy; there was no iron railing at the entrance, no Victoria Street or College Square, no meeting-house nor church, but grassy land on all sides...". By degrees the surroundings cheered up; cricket was played on the lawns, now overlooked by Regency stucco terraces; the Institution became a much-valued townscape component of inner-city Belfast, still imposing viewed up Chichester Street and Wellington Place, with its backdrop of hills. But alas, in 1900 the Governors, in financial straits, sold off the north lawn for £1,350 a year to Belfast Corporation as the site for its massive Technical College: an environmental disaster. Dare one hope that, within the foreseeable future, the Tech might be demolished and the setting of Belfast's only building by a great English architect restored to its pristine state ?

R. CLAYTON, Sc.

The Chapel of Ease (St George's)

Situated in High-street, and erected in the years 1811-12, on the site of an old church taken down in 1777, is an elegant edifice, the portico being one of the most beautiful pieces of architecture in the kingdom.

(THE old early seventeenth-century church was, in fact, demolished in 1774.) A curious hybrid building, built 1811–1813, but only consecrated in 1816: cost £8,820 and could seat 700. Lavens Ewart, in his authoritative book of 1886 on the parishes of the Dioceses of Down, Connor and Dromore says, "St George's was the first Chapel of Ease of Belfast, built on the site previously occupied by the Corporation Church, and in ancient times by the Chapel of the Ford", and adds, most surprisingly at so late a date: "St George's is the only church in the diocese" (of Connor) "in which the services are choral". This tradition no doubt dates back to the 45-year-long incumbency of Canon McIlwaine, originally an evangelical clergyman but later (by Church of Ireland standards) something of a high churchman.

Reading the church from back to front, the chancel, with its murals by Alexander Gibbs, was added in 1882; the main body of the church, with its box-pews and gallery, was originally designed by the Dublin architect John Bowden, but much altered by the Ecclesiastical Commissioners to plans by W J Barre who had died in 1867. But the portico and exterior front wall date from the 1780s, and were transplanted here from Ballyscullion, the palace built by the Earl-Bishop of Derry overlooking the river Bann and Lough Beg. Although Joseph Sandys may have played some part in it, the principal architect of Ballyscullion seems to have been Michael Shanahan of Cork. The central block of the palace, the only part of it ever completed, was elliptical, a fact reflected in the curvature in the front wall of St George's. In November, 1789 the Bishop wrote, over-optimistically, "My House at Ballyscullion…is finished. It is an Oval like the Pantheon, supported and surrounded by 22 Pilasters of the Corinthian order, fluted and 28 feet high. The Portico has six columns 30 feet high of the same Corinthian order.…The offices will be joined to the House by a semicircular colonade like That of St. Peters only closed, because of the Climate". The execution of the stonework was entrusted to David McBlain. Rankin says "Some difficulty was experienced over the carving of the Corinthian capitals. In February 1788 David McBlain maintained that Ballyscullion cut stone" from a quarry near Dungiven "deserved as much as had been paid to his father for work on the Mussenden temple. But although in May McBlain did agree to carve the capitals, whether or not he ever did so is unknown. Alexander Baird was certainly hard at work on them in 1791". And they are certainly very fine.

Having never been completed or occupied, Ballyscullion was dismantled in 1813, ten years after the Bishop's death. His heir had removed most of the contents to Downhill; the chimneypieces and ornamental stonework were then put up for auction. The portico was bought by Dr Nathaniel Alexander, then Bishop of Down and Connor, and presented by him to St George's.

H.NELSON DEL.
F.C.BRUCE.SCULP.

Meeting House, Clarence Street

MAY STREET MEETING HOUSE

Is raised on framed foundations. The front is of modern or Scammozzian Ionic, having two columns and four pilasters, twenty-eight feet high, and fluted. The columns and interior pilasters form a piazza thirty-six feet long, and seven feet wide, over which rises a beautiful pediment. The front of the building is finished with a regular architrave, frieze, and block cornice, which gives it a light, pleasing, and, at the same time, imposing effect. Around the windows are moulded architraves. The entrance is approached by a flight of eight steps, the floor of the building standing considerably above the level of the street. The interior is finished in a superb style. This elegant edifice was erected in the year 1828.

[⁂ "The Meeting-House, Clarence-street [place] *should be "The Meeting-House, May-street"]*

MAY Street Presbyterian church, alas, has suffered much from the degradation of its environment. It used to be surrounded by the handsome late-Georgian terraces of Alfred Street, Hamilton Street, Upper Arthur Street, and May Street itself; opposite stood the excellent classical Victoria Hall, formerly home of the Belfast Anacreontic Society, and the Church of Ireland Diocesan offices in the polychrome style popularised by Ruskin; now nearly all of these, save the Ruskinian (but no longer Diocesan) offices, have been replaced by characterless modern office blocks. Today only the church, a handful of terrace houses in May Street, and another handful in Hamilton Street, survive: but for how much longer ?

The church was especially built for Dr Henry Cooke, a.k.a 'The Black Man', a vociferous cleric and an Orange hero: "a great orator, a matchless debater, an eminent ecclesiastic, a renowned politician, and a chivalrous man" (McConnell), who opened it on 18 October, 1829. "It affords accommodation for 1,700 sitters, and cost upwards of £6,500" (or, perhaps, £9,000)... "The plans from which the building was constructed were those of Mr W. Smith, architect" (otherwise unknown: unless the same person as the builder of the Savings Bank, and of St Mary Magdalene ?)... "The contractor was John Brown, and the amount of the original contract was £4,400, but additions and extras added materially to the cost. The building was very substantially constructed, and the contract was expeditiously carried out."

Vincenzo Scamozzi was a Venetian pupil of Palladio whose seventeenth-century treatise on architecture is, according to Wittkower, "heavy, dogmatic and scholastic": his name used here is a piece of early one-upmanship, signifying little more than that the volutes of the capitals are angled outwards in the Roman manner, rather than flattened in the Greek manner. The interior of the church is rather fine, with good box-pews and gallery.

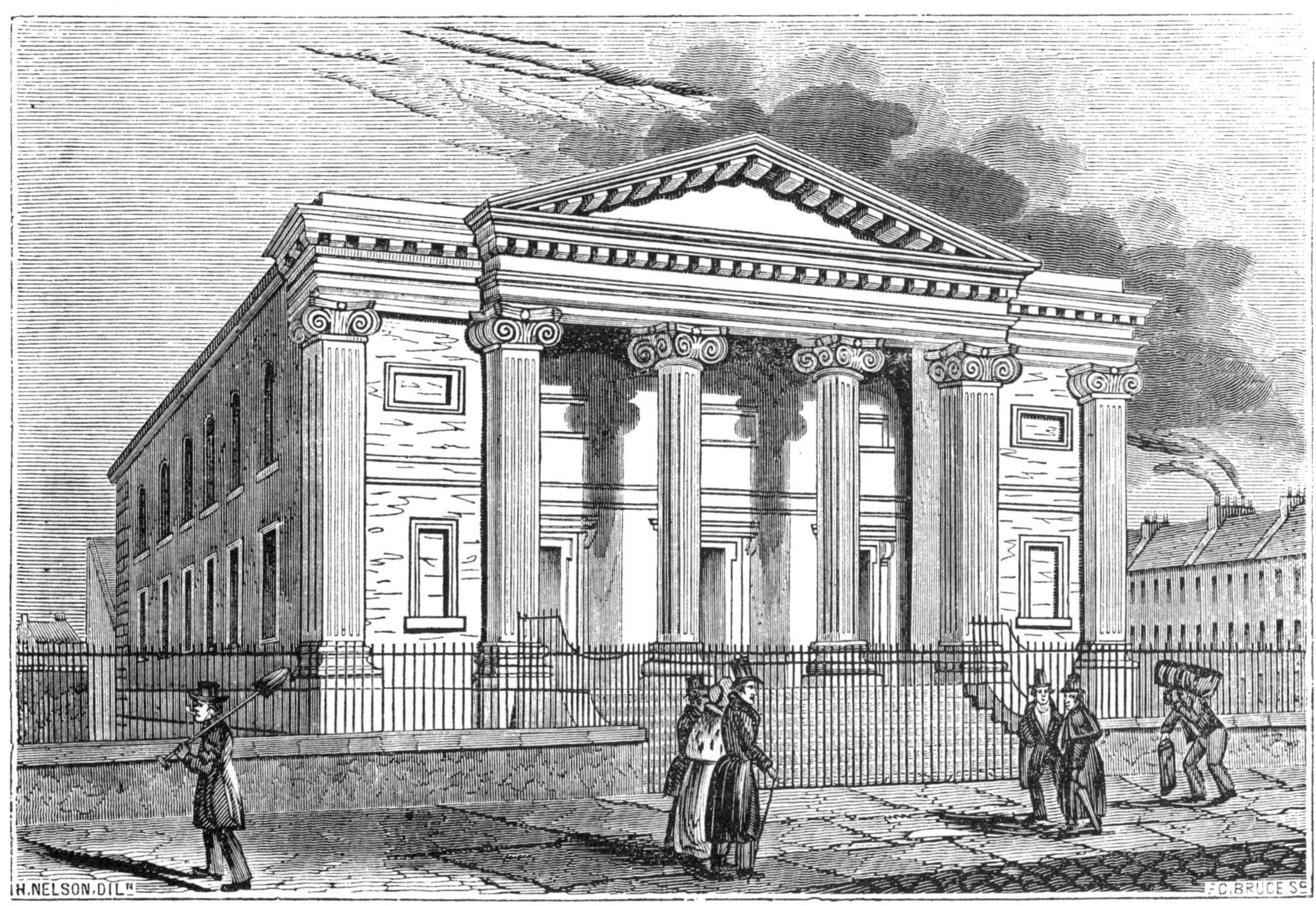
H. NELSON, DIL^N
F.C. BRUCE S^C

Christ Church Meeting House, College Square

It being found that a Church was much wanting for the poorer class of Protestants, the present edifice was erected. The sum of £2,000 was granted by the Board of First Fruits; and £3000 were raised by subscription to complete it. It is a plain edifice, with a cut stone front and colonnade of the Ionic order, surmounted with an entablature; the other parts are of brick, with windows in recesses, ornamented with circular architraves. The interior is laid out to give as much accommodation as possible: there are seats for one thousand persons on the ground-floor; and there is a handsome gallery, which holds upwards of six hundred persons – it has lately been inclosed with an ornamental iron railing. It was opened in July, 1833. Near the Church a most commodious School-House has been erected, which was also completed out of the liberal subscriptions of the inhabitants.

[⁂ What is termed "Christ Church Meeting House, College-square", is not a "Meeting-House", but a "Church"]

THE church, now deconsecrated, has been restored for Inst as the kind of Library, or Information Centre, that contains more computer screens than books. So far as the exterior goes, this is most welcome: as to the interior, doubts may perhaps be permitted. But, of its kind, this is an excellent example of conservation by Belfast Buildings Preservation Trust and Consarc Conservation in 2001-2003, and has received a number of awards.

The original building was consecrated in 1833; may have been built from as early as 1830; designed by William Farrell of Dublin; its first incumbent was the Rev. Thomas Drew, fiery father of the architect Sir Thomas Drew. The church had accommodation for 1,484 persons, of which two-thirds were to be free seats. Lavens Ewart describes it as "a plain, square building, very convenient in every respect, and not at all difficult to fill with the voice". It contained a tremendous three-decker pulpit installed in 1878 by William Batt. In fact, the stone Ionic front, with two Ionic columns in antis, is of monumental simplicity, in Greek Revival style, and makes an extremely important contribution to the streetscape of College Square North.

Unfortunately, this street became known as 'bomb alley' in the 1960s, and by 1985 the church had survived eleven bombs and two arson attacks. Eventually, the vandals were successful; the church was closed, and remained a stark and roofless ruin until its rescue by the Buildings Preservation Trust. It was finally restored, both for the use of the adjacent school and that of the public, with the help of generous support from the Heritage Lottery Fund.

Fisherwick Place Meeting House

Erected in the year 1827-28,is built of polished freestone, of excellent quality; the superstructure resting on a basement of granite-stone, which is elevated above the surface about three feet. On the north and south sides are two ranges of well-proportioned windows, separated by a facia-course, which surrounds the building. The principal entrance is on the west front, which has a handsome portico of the Ionic order, consisting of four columns, and antae, which support a regular entablature and angular pediment. The columns measure twenty-seven feet in height; the capitals of which are imitated from the Ionic temple at Ilissus, near Athens. The entablature of the order is continued along the front of the edifice, supported by antae, over which runs an attic balustrade. The interior of the house, which is well lighted, displays considerable elegance.

GONE. Home of the fifth Presbyterian Congregation of Belfast, always one of the richest and grandest, this church cost £7,000 to build. However, the building of it was not without its vicissitudes. In June, 1824, "the contract for the building of the new church by Mr. James Boyd, Builder, to the plans provided by Mr. Thos.J.Duff, a well-known architect of the time, was signed at a cost of £3,076" (Withers). His six-month contract in fact took three years to complete, at more than double the cost. I know of no better description of it than that set out above. Fisherwick Place was between College Square East and Howard Street, next to the House of Correction on the opposite corner of Howard Street.

It was demolished in 1898, in favour of the new Gothic Revival 'Fisherwick' church on the Malone Road, designed by S P Close, and built 1898 - 1901; the transplanted name has sometimes caused a degree of confusion. The sale of the site to the Presbyterian Assembly for its new headquarters proved no easy matter; the congregation naturally wanted a full and fair price, the negotiators for the Assembly wanted a specially discounted price. It took years to resolve the difference. The new Presbyterian Assembly Building was constructed, not without controversy, to the designs of Young & Mackenzie between 1900 and 1905. It too, in its turn, appears to await an uncertain future: at the date of writing, it seems all too likely that before long either a multi-storey car-park or a multi-storey office block will arise on the site.

H.NELSON.DIL.
F.C.BRUCE.S.

Meeting House, Brown Square

This Building, which was erected during the years 1833-4, is of Grecian architecture. It has wings and a centre in front; and there are four antae or pilasters, two of which stand on the extreme angles of the building, and return on the flanks; surmounted by an entablature from the Chorazic Monument of Thrasyllus; it has also a parapet and acroterice [sic]. The entrance to the body of the house is by three doors in front, having architraves, friezes, and cornices, each finishing with an angular pediment; a belting course runs between the antae, which is surmounted by three sunk pannels having architraves round them; the centre is recessed, and finished in reticulated rustic ashler. The stairs to the galleries rise in the vestibule, to the immediate right and left of the centre door, through which the galleries discharge themselves; and the body of the house is emptied from the two side doors. The entire building is 70 feet in depth by 50 feet in breadth. It belongs to the body of Presbyterians usually denominated "Seceders".

GONE. In fact this church stood, not in Brown Square (now buried underneath the Westlink) but in Townsend Street, looking straight down Brown Street. "On 5th August 1833 Mr. Smyth [could this be William Smith again?] was chosen as Architect, on 17th tenders were received, and on 7th September the estimate of Mr. John Thomson, Newry, for £1,095 was accepted; this price to include a gallery" (McConnell). The church opened for worship in 1835 and was almost immediately extended. But alas, during 1852, "the state of the building had given cause for anxiety. It was clear that the structural work from foundation to ridge had been badly done. The ceiling was reported unsafe, the roof was in constant need of repair, and the foundations were evidently in a bad way." By 1873, however, it was recognised that "The church in which they worshipped…as the committee know to their cost – had been very bady built. The lowest estimate had been taken, and the church spoiled. The joists were laid in the mud, a foot below the level of the street, and had gradually rotted away. The pillars of the gallery were resting upon brickbats, which had also given way – the gallery had sunk – and the roof was in such a condition that some time ago the beams were parting company. In fact, the committee were perpetually tinkering at some part of the building, and spending a good deal of money without anything to show for it" (Johnston). "On the morning of Monday, the 27th November, 1876, the work of demolition began, and in a few days the church of Townsend Street presented, for the first and last time, a striking resemblance to the Temple of Jerusalem – there not being one stone left upon another that was not thrown down."

So, in 1873, it had been resolved to build a new church instead of repairing the old one: Messrs Young & Mackenzie were the architects; "the estimate of Mr William McCammond was accepted – for the church, £6,000, and for the school buildings £2,400." In the end, the total cost of the buildings was £11,200. They were opened in 1878. They narrowly escaped demolition for the Westlink – and are still standing.

The Poor House

An ornamental edifice, with a lofty spire, stands in a very conspicuous elevated situation, at the upper end of Donegal-street. It is an extensive range of building, forming a centre and wings, and was erected by subscription in 1774, for the reception of the aged and infirm, and the support and instruction of destitute children. It regularly maintains and clothes from three to four hundred individuals, young and old.

THAT admirable institution, the Belfast Charitable Society, still flourishes, and administers Clifton House, as the institution is now known; indeed, the buildings between 2001 and 2004 underwent extensive modernisation, repair, and restoration, though the former wards have now been converted into sheltered dwellings, and additional housing has been provided on a site to the rear.

The building, commenced in 1771 and opened in 1774, cost £7,000. It used to be attributed either to Thomas Cooley of Dublin, or to the Scots architect Robert Mylne; but it now seems firmly established that the amateur plans of Robert Joy, a Belfast paper merchant, were those ultimately adopted, though he clearly drew for inspiration on Mylne's drawings. It is of red brick, with stone dressings: a pedimented five-bay central block, with a good pedimented doorcase; four-bay single storey wings with round-headed windows; a pedimented pavilion at either end, with demi-lune window over lesser window in a recess below; all surmounted by tall brick chimney-stacks, and an octagonal stone central spire, with weather-cock. The masons were Joseph McNary, William Anderson, Peter McMeekin and James Brown. The master carpenter was Hugh Dunlap, who modelled a cupola for the building committee as an alternative to the spire: but, rather surprisingly at this date when one might have expected them to have chosen a cupola (or a dome), they made the old-fashioned choice and plumped for the spire. The hall, staircase and assembly room are of some note. Congruous additional wings were added at the rear in 1821, 1825, and 1872. Clifton House is still one of the most important architectural features of Belfast.

The County Institution for Insane Persons

This extensive range of building, situated in the immediate vicinity of the town, a little to the west, arrests the eye for several miles before entering Belfast. It is a well-constructed edifice, admirably fitted for the purposes to which it is devoted – being built after the designs of the various institutions of a similar description erected by Government in different parts of the country. There is a spacious area in front, which serves as a garden and exercise space for the patients.

GONE. It is a pity that the only building in Belfast built to the designs of Francis Johnston, the distinguished architect of Dublin and Armagh, should have been lost. Commenced in 1827 and completed in 1829, in the "healthy air" of the Falls Road, a mile outside the town, and similar to the corresponding institutions built in Armagh and Londonderry. A number of colour-washed elevations are in the Irish Architectural Archive, Dublin, dated 12 March 1827 and bearing the names both of Johnston and of William Murray, his partner, nephew, and successor; since Johnston died in 1829, these buildings were probably executed by Murray. It is said to have cost "upwards of £50,000" *(Parliamentary gazetteer)* and already to have required enlargement by 1836.

The five-bay central block had an elegant cupola, a central portico, and Georgian-glazed windows in recessed panels, all on a semi-basement and broadly similar to the central block of St Luke's Hospital in Armagh. Although shown on Johnston's drawings and in the engraving, the colonnades along the side wings appear not, in fact, to have been executed in Belfast, or for that matter, in Armagh either. Perhaps they were merely intended to provide covered walks – possibly glass-roofed – for the inmates. There were cells for the more gravely afflicted on the ground floor, wards for the convalescents in the larger rooms above.

In 1924, the Asylum was demolished to make way for the new Hospital for Sick Children, a decent but not more distinguished neo-Georgian building completed in 1932 to designs by Tulloch and Fitzsimons.

Natural History Society Museum

The foundation-stone of the building (a front view of which we have given in the engravings, and which stands in College-Square) was laid by the Marquis of Donegall, on the 4th of May, 1830. A bottle, deposited in the first stone, contained the following document:-

MUSEI BELFASTANI
FUNDAMENTA PRIMA
PRAESENTIBUS
SOCIETATIS HISTORIAE NATURALIS APUD BELFASTAM SOCIIS, ALIISQUE MULTIS
SCIENTIAE FAVENTIBUS
QUI AD HOC OPUS PECUNIAM CONTULERANT,
LOCAVIT VIR HONORATISSIMUS
GEORGIUS AUGUSTUS CHICHESTER MARCHIO DE DONEGALL
IV. NON MAIAS MDCCCXXX..
REGE AUGUSTISSIMO GEORGIO IV. ANNUM REGNI XI.

AGENTE – Thoma J. Duff, T. Jackson, Architectis – J. Johnson, redemptore.

In the bottle were also deposited the following articles: - The papers printed at various times by the Belfast Natural History Society; a list of Members of the Society, and Subscribers to the building then about to be commenced; a Belfast Almanack for the year, and the "News-Letter" and "Commercial List" of the day; the coins now current in these kingdoms; an impression of the public seal of the Corporation of the town. The following verses from the 12th chapter of Job, in fifteen different languages – viz. the Hebrew, Greek, Irish, Welsh, Arabic, Latin, Italian, German, Danish, Spanish, Portuguese, French, Romaic, German-Hebrew, and English: -

"Ask now the beasts, and they shall teach thee; and the fowls of the air, and they shall tell thee:
"Or, speak to the earth, and it shall teach thee; and the fishes of the sea shall declare unto thee.
"Who knoweth not in all these that the hand of the Lord hath wrought this ?
"In whose hand is the soul of every living thing, and the breath of all mankind."

A writer in one of the Belfast newspapers, alluding to the circumstance of the time, observed – "If, after the lapse of centuries, the various contents of the bottle should be discovered, and found to be undecayed, the number of languages into which the extract from Job has been translated, would be, perhaps, the most curious and most interesting of its contents. The languages now spoken in Europe will then have undergone many changes, and some may have fallen into disuse; so that the few simple slips of parchment which are now buried in the earth may, like the celebrated Rosetta stone of Egypt, unlock the mysteries of tongues no

longer spoken, and give a key to the interpretation of books and manuscripts, written in languages which have no longer an oral existence." ★

★ *There is not perhaps any public institution in Ireland more interesting in its origin, or honourable to its members and patrons, than the Belfast Natural History Society. It commenced among a few respectable young gentlemen of that town, nearly all of whom were engaged in commercial business, and who devoted those leisure hours to literary and scientific pursuits, which young men of their age and class too generally employ in folly or debauchery. They subscribed a small sum to pay for a room to meet in, and at their meetings curious objects of natural history were exhibited, and original essays were read and commented on. By degrees their numbers increased: young men who attended as visiters merely from feelings of curiosity, became captivated with the delights of knowledge, and zealously applied their minds to its acquisitions. Their proceedings ultimately attracted, as they deserved, the admiration and applause of the older and wealthier citizens of this great commercial town and its vicinity; and a subscription was nobly entered on to procure the youthful society a public edifice for their meetings, and a depository for their valuable museum.*

I am happy to say that, although the collections have since 1917 been transferred to the Belfast (now Ulster) Museum, this handsome building still remains in the ownership of the Belfast Natural History and Philosophical Society; and at present provides a home for the Old Museum Arts Centre.

This, the first Museum in Ireland founded by voluntary subscriptions, was opened in 1831 and was designed by Messrs Duff and Jackson, architects, at a cost of £2,300. According to Pilson, writing in 1846, "the lower storey of this chaste and classic edifice is an imitation of the Choragic Monument of Thrasyllus, with a portico which is an exact copy of that of the octagon tower of Andronicus at Athens; the upper portions after the model of the Temple of Minerva". It is of four storeys, stuccoed and nicely detailed: "The top floor contains a delightfully airy room, lit by three windows and three dome-lights; and surrounded by a railed gallery, to which access is obtained up a curling staircase threaded through a bay supported on three pairs of acanthus-capitalled columns" (Brett, 1967). Alas, the building did not entirely escape the fate of other buildings in this so-called 'bomb alley', and suffered considerable damage in the 1970s. Unhappily, the three dome-lights of that airy upstairs room were not then repaired, but were blocked up, and so remain. It would be a good deed to restore them, and for that matter to restore to more general use this admirable room.

A. Nichol, Esq. del.

Long Bridge across the River Lagan

[previous page]

[Hardy provides no description for this engraving]

GONE. The view looks upriver, with the salt works at Bridge End in Ballymacarrett to the left; the shipping on the right is moored along Donegall Quay. A bridge at this point, to replace the old river ford or 'Long Cross' nearby which gave Belfast its name, was proposed in 1680. It is shown partially built on one of Thomas Phillips's map of 1685, but was finished in the same year. With a roadway nineteen feet wide, the twenty-one arches spanned 840 feet of clear water and provided approach works over the tidal mud-flats on both sides, making a total length of well over half a mile.

Supposedly weakened by the weight of General Schomberg's heavy cannons passing over in 1690, seven arches collapsed in early 1692 but had been rebuilt by the end of the year. Further damage was caused not long afterwards when a ship was blown against the bridge during a storm. Throughout the 18th century there are several mentions of running repairs until, in 1817, it is described as dangerous and "in a state of total insufficiency"; twenty years later Hardy is himself referring to it as "in a tottering condition."

Eventually the Long Bridge was taken down between the summer of 1840 and March 1841 and was replaced by the Queen's Bridge, built by Francis Ritchie to designs by the Antrim and Down County Surveyors, Charles Lanyon and John Frazer.

Distant View of Belfast, from the South

[Hardy provides no description for this engraving]

THE artist's viewpoint is from Newtownbreda: to the left is Richard Cassels's Knockbreda Church of 1737; to the right, in the middle distance, can be seen the distinctive cone-shaped chimneys of the glass works at Bridge End and Short Strand in Ballymacarrett; in the centre is the Long Bridge, with the tower of St Anne's Church standing out against the background of the Cave Hill. A few chimneys of the larger flax-spinning mills are already visible. The two rabbits, going about their business in the foreground, remain oblivious to the sublimity of the scene.

A. Nichol, Esq. del.

Hillsborough

> The town of Hillsborough is finely situated on the summit and sides of a hill, considerably elevated above the surrounding country. It is a very handsome regularly-built town, with a magnificent market-house – a highly-ornamented church, with a lofty spire – an old fort or castle, now appropriated as an armoury for the yeomanry of the town – a neat school-house, and a good inn – the habitations altogether presenting evidences of cleanliness and comfort. It is remarkable as the residence of an Irish nobleman, the Marquis of Downshire.
>
> The Church, which is in the Gothic style, and having a quantity of stained glass in seven of its windows, is said to have cost the late Marquis of Downshire about £15,000 in its erection. It is approached by a long handsome avenue, having a range of full-grown trees on either side . . .

St Malachi's parish church, Hillsborough, is perhaps the most handsome church in the diocese, certainly one of the most elegant and sophisticated. Dr Craig considers that it was this church which, in 1760, "initiated, as far as Ireland is concerned, the gothic revival properly so called". It was built for Wills Hill, Earl of Hillsborough, between 1760 and 1775. His architect is unknown. Various candidates have been put forward: Sanderson Miller, George Richardson, Thomas Wright of Durham, Francis Hiorne of Warwick. All are but guesses. The builders of the very tall, slim, handsome spire are known: they were James and David McBlain. The head mason was Hercules Harper; the joiners William Gardiner and his two sons. As well as woodwork of outstanding quality, the church contains glass after designs by Sir Joshua Reynolds, and a sculpture by Nollekens.

The church itself is in good shape: but, while the lawn and avenue of trees survive, the setting has otherwise been unfortunately degraded by unsightly intrusions.

[Hillsborough Castle]

> ...Hillsborough Castle, an antiquated building in the Marquis of Downshire's park, is remarkable for being the place at which William III. slept, while his army was encamped on Blarish Moor, which is about two miles from Hillsborough, to the left of the Lisburn road, and has been exempt from tithes, &c. since the above period.

Now known as Hillsborough Fort: a castellated garden house built within the ramparts of the seventeenth-century artillery fort, itself built on the site of an earlier rath. Both its date, and its architect, are uncertain; it is said to have been built in 1758, but this has been doubted, and it may be somewhat later; and it has been persuasively conjectured that it was designed by the English gentleman-architect Sanderson Miller.

Rather unhappily "restored" in 1994, when, in an attempt to remedy the pervading damp, the whole building was coated in a hard, cement-based pebble render. "Instead of the agreeably irregular stonework, all surfaces were geometrically flat, and the corner arrises were (and are) as sharp and straight as the knife-edge crease of a bank manager's trousers. The glowing golden colour of the stonework has been replaced by a uniform grey. The Fort now appears, to some at least, rather dreary, suburban and charmless" (Brett, 1995).

Drum Church

Stands on an eminence, in a fertile and well-wooded part of the country, on the banks of the Lagan, and convenient to the old road leading from Belfast to Lisburn; four miles from the former, and three from the latter place. The scenery along the river side to Lisburn is extremely beautiful and picturesque, and might probably make the difference of about a mile.

Now Drumbeg: Saint Patrick's. Lewis says "the church was rebuilt by subscription in 1798, by the aid of a gift of £461 from the Board of First Fruits: it has a tower surmounted by a spire, which having been blown down in 1831, was rebuilt at the expense of J. Charley, Esq." The rebuilding took place in 1833. The original spire had been wooden, but it was rebuilt in stone. Lavens Ewart says, "The interesting and picturesque steeple of the old church remains, built about 1784 [*sic: recte,* 1798]; the site on the summit of Drum Hill; church cruciform.... A tablet in the tower porch states that Drumbeg Church was rebuilt in 1798. The church was rebuilt in 1870, the tower and spire being preserved". The rebuilt body of the church was designed by Sir Thomas Drew.

The church is of moderate interest; it has a lych-gate, often mis-spelled, of 1878; but the graveyard is charming: in it lie the remains of many of my old friends. The bridge gives access to the paths alongside the River Lagan and the Lagan canal.

Forth Bridge

Is situated on the river Lagan, about three miles from Lisburn, and forms a picturesque object in the landscape.

ACTUALLY situated not on the river itself, but on the Lagan canal. For 'Forth' read 'Fourth': the first bridge over the canal was at Newforge; the second at Shaw's Bridge; the third at Drumbeg; so this one was the fourth. Built between 1759 and 1763 by Thomas Omer, canal engineer, as an element in only the second canal in the British Isles. "The original road from Belfast to Lisburn here crosses the canal, at a high level, over a curious S-shaped path. There are two semi-circular stone arches, one broad (over the canal), one narrow (over the tow-path). The bridge is of squared, reddish, sandstone, with two string-courses" (Brett, 2002).

Fred Hamond remarks, "wear marks of the barge tow ropes are visible along the edges of the central pier... Historically it is of interest on account of its mid-eighteenth century construction date.... Architecturally, it is arguably the most impressive canal bridge, in terms of scale and proportion, to survive in the province. Finally, it makes a very significant impact on the landscape hereabouts."

The lock-keeper's house, well restored by HEARTH in 1992-3, stands on the hill-top nearby; there are no less than 34 steps down the cutting to the canal – and up again, after the barge might have passed through the eighth lock of the Lagan canal. Unfortunately, trees and scrub have now grown so verdantly up the banks of the cutting that it is impossible to gain a clear view, or for that matter a photograph, of what is now known as the Ballyskeagh High Bridge.

Ruins of Grey Abbey, County of Down

This once celebrated abbey was situated in the vicinity of a small town of the same name, about ten miles from Belfast, and within a short distance of Strangford Lough. The ruins are of considerable extent, in good preservation, and finely situated for effect.

FOUNDED in 1193 by Affreca, wife of John de Courcy, and colonised by Cistercian monks from Cumberland. Built in a very Anglo-Norman style by English craftsmen, some of whom left their masons' marks, its lands farmed largely by English lay brothers. Stalley says "Grey Abbey has a good claim to be considered the first Gothic building in Ireland… To the frontiers of European civilisation, to Brittany, Sweden, Poland, Wales and Ireland, the Cistercians brought the basic elements of Romanesque and Gothic design: clear principles of planning, well-proportioned, well-buttressed structures, along with excellent standards of construction".

The abbey was dissolved in 1541; in 1572 its remains were burned by Sir Brian O'Neill to prevent their use by the English invaders of the Ards. The nave was re-roofed in the seventeenth century and served as parish church until 1778.

The ruins are in good shape, well cared for, and stand in a delightful setting.

A. NICHOLL. DIL.
J. BRUCE. SC

Lord O'Neill's Cottage, Ram's Island

This pretty little cottage is situated in one of the small islands of Lough Neagh, at a distance of three miles from Crumlin, and about one mile and two-thirds from the shore, from which the traveller can easily procure a boat for the purpose of visiting the island. The cottage, furnished in the most tasteful manner, was some years since erected by Earl O'Neill, to whom it belongs. The only object of antiquity is a round tower, of which

—*"Time, with assailing arm,*
Hath smote the summit, but the solid base
Derides the lapse of ages."

We are informed by the Rev. Doctor Cupples, that its height is forty-three feet, its circumference thirty feet five inches, the thickness of the walls two feet eight inches and a quarter; the first story contains the door – the second, a window facing the south-east – and the third, another window, which looks out to the north, about three feet high, and one and a half broad. The entire ground is laid out in walks, and covered with verdure. Several hundred rose trees, and those plants and flowers which constitute the pride of our gardens, all flourish luxuriantly. Even those sides of the island which are almost perpendicular, are adorned with all those creeping plants and hardy shrubs which are adapted to the situation.

THE stump of the round tower still stands, although with a gaping hole in the stonework: the cottage and gardens, alas, have quite vanished, and the island is now a self-sown jungle of vegetation. According to H C Lawlor, this island was "anciently known as Inis-Garden" (*Preliminary survey of the ancient monuments of Northern Ireland*), which is certainly a nice thought. It is believed to have been an early monastic site.

The cottage on the island was said to have been bought by Lord O'Neill from a Liverpool merchant named James Whittle; and to have been accidentally burned down during the second World War by a group of visitors, airmen from the nearby American base at the Langford Lodge aerodrome. A local group of enthusiasts has recently undertaken to try to restore the island, and its long-abandoned gardens, to better order.

A. Nichol, Esq. del.

Shane's Castle

Situated on the north-east shore of Lough Neagh, for centuries the family seat of the noble house of O'Neill, was burned to the ground, by an accidental fire, in the year 1816. The following description of the place, as it appeared prior to the fire, was communicated, with the drawing, by Colonel de Montmorency, for the "Dublin Penny Journal":

"The annexed sketch represents the principal, though least picturesque front of the Castle, which stands in the centre of a splendid park, richly ornamented with large timber trees, and young plantations – the rere and lateral portions of the edifice commanding a boundless view over the far-famed Lough Neagh. The elevation of Shane's Castle partakes of the modern castellated Gothic – which style, although inferior in many respects, to the primitive gloomy, yet *ever sublime* Gothic of the 12th and 13th centuries, will be esteemed, nevertheless, an architectural form much more characteristic of a proud baronial manor – turreted – embattled – in the plenitude and full display of feudal pomp and power, than any thing borrowed from, or mixed up with, the Greek and Roman orders could or ought to produce.

"At the period I had visited Shane's Castle, workmen were busily employed on the erection of a range of handsome buildings, in corresponding style with the mansion, destined to effect a nearer approach between the latter and the lake. The Earl O'Neill, I was told, had also in contemplation to surround his *chateau* with a fosse, draw-bridges, &c. The prominent features of the manor were demonstrative rather of durability, convenience, and internal comfort, than magnificence: the apartments neither on a large scale nor lofty, but numerous, and so distributed and furnished as to leave on the visiter's mind a favourable notion of the hospitality of the owner.

"Midst the ruins of a decayed church, accompanied by the weepings, wailings, and sad lamentations, not only of the men of Antrim and of all Ulster, but to the unspeakable grief and sorrow of every well-wisher of his country, were interred, with those of his ancestors, the *murdered* remains of the Right Hon. John O'Neill, first Viscount O'Neill of Shane's Castle. The circumstances of his death were as follows: -

After the breaking out of the disastrous insurrection of 1798, (fomented and got up by persons, and for purposes, now well known,) Lord O'Neill, truly anxious to prevent the effusion of human blood, and, if possible, save the country from exposure to the destructive consequences of civil war – but, unfortunately, at the same time too rashly confiding in the strength and power of his own popularity, and the hereditary influence of his great name – at the critical moment when the king's troops and the insurgents were already, *en presence,* in battle array before the town of Antrim, had the hardihood, or indiscretion, regardless, and, indeed, unapprehensive of danger, or of any possible insult being offered to him, to ride forward, singly and unattended, and placing himself in the centre between the two lines of menacing combatants, commence making a peace-exhorting harangue to, as he erroneously supposed, the wavering mass of insurgents:when a dastard sanguinary wretch, armed with a pike, rushed suddenly from a cabin close by, followed by a companion

(From the Collection of Colonel H. de Montmorency)

similarly accoutred, and advancing suddenly upon his Lordship, piked his horse, at the same instant that the accomplice plunged his merciless weapon into the victim's breast. Thus perished by the assassin's hand one of the noblest of Erin's sons! – one of the chief members of that illustrious patriot phalanx of 1782, whose names shall descend to the latest posterity, and distinguish the age they lived in! The people of Antrim, with many of whom I conversed upon the subject upon the theatre of the action – who had themselves played prominent parts, before and since that day, in the ranks of the insurgents, and participated in the victory obtained by the royalist forces for their party – they one and all assured me that O'Neill's murderers were disowned and disavowed, as well by the insurgents, as the sedentary portion of that time of the inhabitants of Antrim, to whom they were personally unknown."

Ruins of Shane's Castle

From the ruins which remain, it is evident that it was a fine spacious building: the vaults, which are still entire, and extend to the very verge of the lake, merit the particular notice of the curious traveller, both from their great spaciousness and rather extraordinary construction. Several turrets and towers are still standing; and from their tops a fine view of the interesting scenery amid which the ruins lie, may be obtained. A number of cannons are still mounted on the fort, which is boldly situated. Some of the buildings which formed a part of the out-offices, have been fitted up by the noble proprietor as a temporary residence. We have heard with pleasure, that it is his Lordship's intention to erect a castle, if not on the ruins of the old one, on some spot in the immediate vicinity. An extensive library and many valuable paintings were wholly consumed in this awful conflagration; the green-house, or grand conservatory of rare and foreign plants, being the only thing that escaped.

THE picturesque ruins of the first Shane's Castle, of uncertain date, still stand close to the original shoreline; but now at some distance from it as the result of successive lowerings of the level of the Lough. An intermediate Shane's Castle was built to designs by Charles Lanyon in 1862, but destroyed by another fire, this time deliberately started by Sinn Fein, in 1922. The present house was built further inland for the current Lord O'Neill in 1958 to designs by Arthur Jury.

The turrets and the cannons are still there, as are the very extensive tunnels, passages, store-rooms and great basement kitchen underneath the terrace. The "green-house, or grand conservatory", built by John Nash between 1812 and 1816 when he was working at Killymoon Castle, was originally filled with "rare exotics, besides some remarkably fine orange and lemon trees" but is now known as 'The Camellia House', and filled with very fine mature camellias of a number of different varieties: a sight worth seeing when they are in flower.

A. Nichol, Esq. del.

Antrim Round Tower

About a mile from Antrim, in a north-east direction, stands this fine specimen of these ancient buildings. It is 95 feet in height, 52 feet in girth, near the base, and about 36 near the top. About 18 feet from its top it tapers in form of a sugar-loaf. At the ground are two circles of stones, projecting about eight inches – nine feet above which is a small opening or door-way, facing to the north, to which there are no steps or other way of ascending. It is perfectly round both internally and externally, and apparently but little impaired by time. There are three tiers of loop-holes – those near the top are round, and correspond with the cardinal points. Inside are places in the walls for resting beams, so as to form the different stories of the building. The wall is upwards of three feet thick.

STILL standing, and in excellent order. "A 10th or 11th century date seems likely" (*Historic monuments of Northern Ireland*). All that survives of a formerly extensive monastic site, perhaps connected with St Comgall. It is perhaps surprising that the Dublin Penny Journal does not attribute this monument to the Gobhan Saer, or 'Gobban the Builder', as does its regular contributor, Samuel M'Skimin of Carrickfergus, in 1833; who says the Goban was a woman: and that he/she brewed an ale which kept all who partook thereof from illness and death. George Petrie, too, in 1845, attributes this tower to "the celebrated architect, Goban, or, as he is popularly called, Goban Saer, who flourished early in the seventh century... the son of a skilful artisan in wood, if not in stone also...if not a foreigner, at least probably of foreign extraction, and that the Goban himself was very probably born at Turvy, on the northern coast of the County of Dublin..." Steeple House can be seen to the rear.

A. NICHOLL. ESQ.
CLAYTON Sc

Lisburn

About nine miles from Belfast is the large and populous town of Lisburn, supposed to be the second town for size and commerce in the county of Antrim, containing about 1000 houses, and about five times that number of inhabitants. The streets are well laid out – the houses in general of an excellent description, and having a handsome appearance. The church has a lofty steeple, and there is an ornamental cupola on the market-house. Altogether, the town presents a gratifying appearance of industry and prosperity. The linen and diaper manufacture is carried on very extensively, and some of the finest and most beautiful pieces of diaper ever produced in Ireland have been manufactured here, by the descendants of French refugees.

CHRIST Church, the Church of Ireland cathedral of the Diocese of Connor since 1662, has indeed a tall, slim, elegant spire, octagonal, with three roll-mouldings at its base, added at a cost of £1500 in 1804 by that excellent stonemason David McBlain of Limavady to the tower of 1674, which unlike the nave of about 1645 had survived the great fire of 1707. This started in the cathedral and eventually destroyed most of the town, together with the neighbouring castle. The body of the church was rebuilt from 1708 onwards. It is still a fine building, in very good shape, and marks out from a considerable distance the heart of the town.

The very sophisticated cupola of the former market-house, with its coupled Corinthian columns at the four corners, and the splendid Assembly Rooms, both of around 1707, survive; there are very few eighteenth-century assembly rooms of equal merit in Ulster which remain – alas, Sir Robert Taylor's Assembly Rooms in Belfast have long since succumbed. "The Lisburn ladies have long been proverbial for beauty" – perhaps they still are. In 1834, a gymnasium and a lending library were added to the Assembly Rooms; then various other nineteenth-century excrescences. Now home of the excellent Irish Linen Centre and Lisburn Museum: but externally, the late twentieth-century additions and extensions, whilst having attracted numerous awards, mingle the old and the modern in a way which at least some observers find unduly aggressive.

There are still a few good buildings in Castle Street and the town centre; but to a large extent, the old Lisburn has gone for ever, along with the linen and diaper industries.

S4ORE
R.CLAYTON. S^c

Bibliography

An archaeological survey of County Down. Ed. by E.M.Jope, Belfast, 1966

Bardon, Jonathan *An interesting and honourable history: the Belfast Charitable Society, the first 250 years, 1752–2002*, Belfast, 2002

Barry, John *Hillsborough: a parish in the Ulster Plantation.* 3rd ed., Belfast, 1982

Batt, Narcissus 'Belfast sixty years ago: recollections of a septuagenarian', in *Ulster Journal of Archaeology,* 2nd series, 2, 1896, pp 92–95

Benn, George *The history of the town of Belfast...and a description of some remarkable antiquities in its neighbourhood.* Belfast, 1823

Benn, George *A history of the town of Belfast from the earliest times to ...1810.* 2 vols, London, 1877–1880

Benn, George 'Reminiscences of Belfast', in *Ulster Journal of Archaeology,* 1st series, 3, 1855, pp 260–64; 5, 1857, pp 144–50

Blair, May *Once upon the Lagan: the story of the Lagan canal.* Rev. ed., Belfast, 2000

Brett, C. E. B. 'Brett on the Hillsborough Fort controversy', in *Ulster Architect*, 12, 1995, pp 8–9

Brett, C. E. B. *Buildings of Belfast,* 1700–1914. Rev. ed., Belfast, 1985

Brett, C. E. B. *Buildings of County Antrim,* Belfast, 1996

Brett, C. E. B. *Buildings of north County Down,* Belfast, 2002

Brett, C. E. B. *Court houses and market houses of the province of Ulster,* Belfast, 1973

Brett, C. E. B. *Georgian Belfast, 1750–1850: maps, buildings and trades* (Irish historic towns atlas), Dublin, 2004

Brett, C. E. B. 'The Georgian town: Belfast about 1800' in Beckett, J. C. and Glasscock, R. E., eds *Belfast: the origin and growth of an industrial city,* London, 1967

Brett, C. E. B. *Roger Mulholland, architect of Belfast 1740–1818,* Belfast, 1976

Brett, C. H. Notes on the topography of old Belfast: talk delivered to Belfast Literary Society, 5 December 1870. Typescript in possession of C. E. B. Brett

Carmody, W. P. *Lisburn Cathedral and its past rectors,* Belfast, 1926

Clergy of Down and Dromore. Ed. and with brief parish histories by Fred Rankin, Belfast, 1996

Clyde, Tom *Irish literary magazines: an outline history and descriptive bibliography,* Dublin, 2003

Craig, Maurice *The architecture of Ireland,* London, 1982

Curl, J. S. *Classical churches in Ulster,* Belfast, 1980

Deane, Arthur, ed., *The Belfast Natural History and Philosophical Society. Centenary volume 1821–1921: a review of the activities of the Society for 100 years with historical notes, and memoirs of many distinguished members*, Belfast, 1924

Dixon, Hugh 'Honouring Thomas Jackson, 1807–1890 (Architect)', in *Proceedings and Reports of the Belfast Natural History and Philosophical Society,* 2nd series, 9, 1970/71–1976/77, pp 23–31

Dixon, Hugh *Soane and the Belfast Academical Institution,* Ballycotton, 1976

Doyle, J. B., *Tours in Ulster: a handbook to the antiquities and scenery of the north of Ireland,* Dublin, 1854

Ewart, L. M. *Handbook to the United Diocese of Down & Connor & Dromore,* Belfast, [1886]

Gaffikin, Thomas *Belfast fifty years ago. A lecture delivered...1875.* 3rd ed., Belfast, 1894

Galloway, Peter *The cathedrals of Ireland,* Belfast, 1992

Gillespie, Raymond and Royle, S. A. *Belfast. Part I, to 1840* (Irish historic towns atlas, 12), Dublin, 2003

H, J.J. 'Belfast's many bridges and their historic associations', in *Belfast Telegraph,* 6/2/1931

Hall, S. C . and Hall, A. M. *Ireland: its scenery, character, &c.* 3 vols, London, 1841–1843

Hamond, F. W. *Antrim coast & glens: industrial heritage,* Belfast, 1991

Hardy, P. D. *The northern tourist, or stranger's guide to the north and north west of Ireland,* Dublin, 1830

Hayes, James 'Old popular pennyworths', in *Irish Book Lover,* 2, 1911, pp 149–51

Hayley, Barbara 'A reading and thinking nation: periodicals as the voice of nineteenth-century Ireland', in Hayley, Barbara and McKay, Enda, eds., *Three hundred years of Irish periodicals,* Gigginstown, Mullingar, 1987

Hearth, *A review of projects 1999,* Belfast, 1999

Historic monuments of Northern Ireland. Ed. by Ann Hamlin, Belfast, 1983

A history of congregations in the Presbyterian Church in Ireland 1610-1982, Belfast, 1982

Jamieson, John *The history of the Royal Belfast Academical Institution, 1810–1960,* Belfast, 1959 [i.e. 1960]

Johnston, W. *A memorial sketch of Townsend Street Presbyterian Church,* Belfast, 1880

Killen, John *A history of the Linen Hall Library 1788–1988,* Belfast, 1990

Larmour, Paul *Belfast: an illustrated architectural guide,* Belfast, 1987

Lawson, J. P. *The gazetteer of Ireland containing the latest information from the most authentic sources,* Edinburgh, 1842

Lee, Nicholas, ed. *Irish identity and literary periodicals 1832–1842*. 6 vols, Bristol, 2000

Lewis, Samuel *A topographical dictionary of Ireland*. 3 vols, London, 1837; 2nd ed., 1847

McConnell, James *Presbyterianism in Belfast,* Belfast, 1912

MacNeice, J. F. *The Church of Ireland in Belfast: its growth, condition, needs; the story of the churches 1778–1931,* Belfast, 1931

McParland, Edward *Francis Johnston, architect, 1760-1829,* Celbridge, 1969 (Quarterly Bulletin of the Irish Georgian Society, 12, Nos 3/4)

McTear, Thomas 'Personal recollections of the beginning of the century', in *Ulster Journal of Archaeology,* 2nd series, 5, 1898–9, pp 67–80, 162–74, 211-13

Maguire, W. A. 'Absentees, architects and agitators: the fifth Earl of Donegall and the building of Fisherwick Place', in *Proceedings and Reports of the Belfast Natural History and Philosophical Society*, 2nd series, 10, 1977/78–1981/82, pp 5–21

Morton, R. G. 'The Charitable Institution, Belfast' in *Quarterly Bulletin of the Irish Georgian Society,* 4, 1961, pp 17–21

Neill, Matthew *Ecclesia de Drum: recollections of the parish of Drumbeg, Diocese of Down,* Belfast, [1995]

Nesbitt, Noel *A museum in Belfast: a history of the Ulster Museum and its predecessors,* Belfast 1979

O'Keefe, Peter and Simington, Tom *Irish stone bridges: history and heritage,* Dublin 1991

The parliamentary gazetteer of Ireland. 3 vols, Dublin, 1845–1846

Patton, Marcus *Central Belfast: a historical gazetteer,* Belfast, 1993

Petrie, George *The ecclesiastical architecture of Ireland anterior to the Anglo-Norman invasion,* Dublin, 1845

Pilson, J. A. *History of the rise and progress of Belfast, and annals of the county of Antrim,* Belfast, 1846

A preliminary survey of the ancient monuments of Northern Ireland. Ed. by D. A. Chart, Belfast, 1940

Rankin, P. J. *Irish building ventures of the Earl Bishop of Derry 1730-1803,* Belfast, 1972

Scott, E.V. *Churches of the Diocese of Connor: an illustrated history,* [Newtownabbey?, 1997]

Smith, J. H. *Belfast and its environs, with a tour to the Giant's Causeway.* 2nd ed., Dublin, 1853

[Smyth, John] 'Belfast sixty years ago [ca 1808]. By an Octogenarian'. Ed. by J. J. Marshall, in *Belfast Telegraph,* 26/9/1934–12/12/1934, 18/11/1936–23/12/1936

Stalley, Roger *The Cistercian monasteries of Ireland: an account of the history, art and architecture of the white monks in Ireland 1142–1540,* London, 1987

Strain, R. W. M. *Belfast and its Charitable Society: a story of urban social development,* London, 1961

Strickland, W. G. *A dictionary of Irish artists.* 2 vols, Dublin, 1913

[Thackeray, W. M.] *The Irish sketch-book. By Mr M. A. Titmarsh*. 2 vols, London, 1843

Views in Belfast, [Dublin, 1833] (Supplement to *Dublin Penny Journal,* 1, 1832/33)

Views in the neighbourhood of Belfast, [Dublin, 1836] (Supplement to *Dublin Penny Journal,* 4, 1835/36)

Walker, Simon *Historic Ulster churches,* Belfast, 2000

Webb, Alfred *A compendium of Irish biography,* Dublin, 1878

Williamson, John *May Street Presbyterian Church centenary: a history of the congregation,* Belfast, 1929

Withers, John *Our past years: Fisherwick Church, Belfast, 1823–1973,* Belfast, [1974]

Wittkower, Rudolf *Art and architecture in Italy 1600-1750*. Rev. ed., Harmondsworth, 1982

Young, J. A. *Unfinished pilgrimage: the story of Belfast Cathedral,* Belfast, [1945]